COYOTE'S CANYON

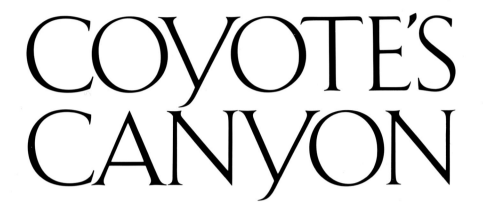

COYOTE'S CANYON

Photographs by
JOHN TELFORD
Stories by
TERRY TEMPEST WILLIAMS

GIBBS·SMITH
P
PUBLISHER

PEREGRINE SMITH BOOKS
SALT LAKE CITY

04 03 02 01 12 11 10

Photographs copyright © John Telford

Text copyright © Terry Tempest Williams. "Lion Eyes" appeared in *Petroglyph*. "Kokopelli's Return" appeared in *Backpacker*. "The Stone Spiral" appeared in *Shandoka*. "The Bowl" appeared in *North American Review*.

Published by
Gibbs Smith, Publisher, P.O. Box 667, Layton, Utah 84041

Design by J. Scott Knudsen

Printed and bound by Sung in Printing Co., Ltd.

in Korea

Cover photos © John Telford:

Anasazi Pictograph, Grand Gulch, Utah
Echo Canyon, Zion National Park, Utah.

Library of Congress Cataloging-in-Publication Data
Telford, John. 1944-
    Coyote's canyon / photographs by John Telford, stories by Terry Tempest Williams.
        p.   cm.
    ISBN 0-87905-245-7 : (pbk)
    1. Utah—Description and travel—1981- —
Views. 2. National parks and reserves—Utah—
Pictorial works. 3. Natural history—Utah—Pictorial
works. I. Williams, Terry Tempest.   II. Title.
F827.T45   1989
917.92—dc19   88-39386
                                          CIP

ACKNOWLEDGMENTS

PHOTOGRAPHS taken over a period of more than a decade cannot be made without help, influence and encouragement from many people. At the risk of leaving some out, I seek to remember them all. Al Taylor and Tom Haslam generously took me to many of the places where photographs could be made, and also taught me to laugh at myself. Chris and Erica Wangsgard introduced the wilderness to me, and together with friends like Bruce Hucko, taught me to go beyond self-imposed limitations. Al Weber, Philip Hyde, Eliot Porter, Ed Riddell, Jon Stuart, and numerous other photographers have given needed criticism and encouragement to fuel the creative fires that dwindle frequently over many years.

I am grateful to my students who have looked and listened and, above all, forced me to articulate my photographs and thoughts, thereby clarifying them to myself.

And certainly without support of family and loved ones, this labor of love would have died a premature death. My dear wife, Valerie, and my five children have given up much so that I might pursue a dream.

JT

A STORY is always a journey and I have had extraordinary companions: Glen Lathrop, Bruce Hucko, Chris Noble, Tom Till, Thea Nordling, and Nancy Shanaman. Mary Gesicki, Ann Hanniball, and Lynne Tempest imagined these stories with me. They are sisters. Robin Wilson and Karla VanderZanden elucidated the canyon country through their passion for the Canyonlands Field Institute in Moab, Utah. Winston Hurst, Fred Blackburn, and Larry Davis are role models for how one lives well in southern Utah. And Jim Hepworth, Jeri McAndrews, Anne Milliken, and Robley Wilson, Jr., gifted me with their perceptions. To all of these desert friends, I am grateful.

And a special debt must be paid to the public relations firm of Peacock, Abbey, Foreman and Sanders for tutelage in desert etiquette.

Mary and Gene Fousheé provided refuge, making Bluff, Utah, a destination, just as Jane and Ken Sleight made Pack Creek home in Moab. And I want to thank Opal Hooper and Gracie and Ray Hunt, who keep the stories that circulate around trading posts alive.

Carl Brandt came to the desert to see if these stories were true. He kept us honest. To him, I am indebted. My grandmother, Kathryn B. Tempest, is the storyteller I listen to. It is she who understands the unseen world.

And to Brooke Williams, the "Lion of Zion," I acknowledge his gift of exploration. Without him, I would never have found Coyote's Canyon or had the desire to return home.

TTW

GIBBS SMITH pushed the boundaries of our imagination and showed us what is possible. Scott Knudsen took images and gave them form. James Thomas corraled the stories with care, as Madge Baird held the line and made the imagined real. To them and the staff of Gibbs Smith, we are indebted.

JOHN TELFORD
TERRY TEMPEST WILLIAMS

A PHOTOGRAPHER'S NOTE

IN 1969, when I first saw Eliot Porter's photographs of Glen Canyon in *The Place No One Knew*, I was sure the printer had manipulated the presses to create the magical colors. Colors like that don't exist in nature, I thought. After all, I am from Utah—I ought to know. In 1972, when I made my first trip to the flooded remains of Glen Canyon–Lake Powell, I caught a glimpse of just how intense the colors really are. Now, having photographed in the desert canyons for more than sixteen years, I realize that the printer couldn't do justice to Porter's photographs.

Absorbed in the solitude of sandstone corridors, I began to look and see and feel the energy of the light. It's not the color of the canyons, but rather the color of the light, that permeates the rocks and brings them to life. In the open shade of towering walls, there is no direct sunlight. Instead, the sun illuminates a wall on the opposite side of the canyon, and that light, infused with the intrinsic warm colors of the sandstone wall, is reflected into the open shade, there combining with the reflected blue of sapphire skies. It is this reflected light, amplified in color with each recoil, which brings the desert to life.

The light begins to suggest qualities and objects that, in reality, don't exist, and imagination begins to see possibilities beyond mesozoic eolian sandstone. The canyons become a sanctuary of secrets begging to be told. And suddenly one feels a kinship with the culture that left these canyons some eight hundred to a thousand years ago.

With that in mind, knowing that these photographs, with rare exception, were taken with a thirty-five-year-old Deardorff camera adds little meaning. The fact that Ektachrome and Fujichrome films were used is as unimportant as knowing what brand of paint was used by Picasso. And as for exposure data, each sheet of film was adequately exposed. The only really important thing to consider is content.

When walking through the canyons, I see form, shape, line and texture as revealed by light and color. Objects are not important as such, but rather as shape. Shape juxtaposed with shape becomes a composition—a found composition. The photographer merely has to recognize the composition and capture it on the ground glass. In this land of light, rocks are elevated to sculpture, and each earth gesture is a work of art.

JOHN TELFORD
October 1988

CONTENTS

"These things are real:

desert,

rocks,

shelter,

legend."

JUDITH FRYER

From *The Desert is No Lady*,
edited by Janice Monk and
Vera Norwood, Yale
University Press, 1987

COYOTE'S CANYON

THE COYOTE CLAN

When traveling to southern Utah for the first time, it is fair to ask if the redrocks were cut would they bleed. And when traveling to Utah's desert for the second or third time, it is fair to assume that they do, that the blood of the rocks gives life to the country. And then after having made enough pilgrimages to the slickrock to warrant sufficient separation from society's oughts and shoulds, look again for the novice you once were, who asks if sandstone bleeds.

Pull out your pocketknife, open the blade, and run it across your burnished arm. If you draw blood, you are human. If you draw wet sand that dries quickly, then you will know you have become part of the desert. Not until then can you claim ownership.

This is Coyote's country — a landscape of the imagination, where nothing is as it appears. The buttes, mesas, and redrock spires beckon you to see them as something other: a cathedral, a tabletop, bears' ears, or nuns. Windows and arches ask you to recall what is no longer there, to taste the wind for the sandstone it carries. These astonishing formations invite a new mythology for desert goers, one that acknowledges the power of story and ritual, yet lies within the integrity of our own cultures. The stories rooted in experience become beads to trade. It is the story, always the story, that precedes and follows the journey.

Just when you begin to believe in your own sense of place, plan on

Wall detail, Kolob Canyon, Zion National Park, Utah.

16

getting lost. It's not your fault—blame it on Coyote. The terror of the country you thought you knew bears gifts of humility. The landscape that makes you vulnerable also makes you strong. This is the bedrock of southern Utah's beauty: its chameleon nature according to light and weather and season encourages us to make peace with our own contradictory nature. The trickster quality of the canyons is Coyote's cachet.

When the Navajos speak of Coyote, they do so hesitantly, looking over their shoulders, checking the time of year so they won't be heard. They know his stories are told only after the first frost and never after the last thaw. Their culture has been informed by Coyote. He is profane and sacred, a bumbler and a hero. He straddles the canyon walls with wild oats in his belly. And they know him by name—Ma'ii, the one never to be taken for granted. They understand his fickle nature, how he seduces fools into believing their own myths, that they matter to the life of the desert.

Coyote knows we do not matter. He knows rocks care nothing for those who wander through them; and yet he also knows that those same individuals who care for the rocks will find openings—large openings—that become passageways into the unseen world, where music is heard through doves' wings and wisdom is gleaned from the tails of lizards. Coyote is always nearby, but remains hidden. He is an ally because he cares enough to stay wary. He teaches us how to survive.

It is Coyote who wanders naked in the desert and leaves his skin on the highway, allowing us to believe he is dead. He knows sunburned flesh is better than a tanned hide, that days spent in the desert are days soaking up strength. He can retrieve his coat and fluff up his fur after a wild day in the wilderness and meet any man, woman, or child on the streets of Moab and seduce them for dinner. Coyote knows it is the proportion of days spent in wildness that counts in urbane savvy.

Coyote's howl above the canyon says the desert may not depend on his life, but his life depends on the desert.

We would do well to listen.

The canyons of southern Utah are giving birth to a Coyote Clan— hundreds, maybe even thousands, of individuals who are quietly subversive on behalf of the land. And they are infiltrating our neighborhoods in the most respectable ways, with their long, bushy tails tucked discreetly inside their pants or beneath their skirts.

Members of the Clan are not easily identified, but there are clues. You can see it in their eyes. They are joyful and they are fierce. They can cry louder and laugh harder than anyone on the planet. And they have enormous range.

The Coyote Clan is a raucous bunch: they have drunk from desert potholes and belched forth toads. They tell stories with such virtuosity that you'll swear you have been in the presence of preachers.

The Coyote Clan is also serene. They can float on their backs down the length of any river or lose entire afternoons in the contemplation of stone.

Members of the Clan court risk and will dance on slickrock as flash floods erode the ground beneath their feet. It doesn't matter. They understand the earth re-creates itself day after day.

The images and stories to follow come from Coyote's Canyon. They are dedicated to the Clan, to give them strength when they are away from the slickrock, to jar their memories that beauty is not found in the excessive, but in what is lean and spare and subtle.

TERRY TEMPEST WILLIAMS
October 1988

Towers of the Virgin, Zion National Park, Utah.

Temple of the Sun and Moon, Cathedral Valley, Capitol Reef National Park, Utah.

Coyote Canyon, Escalante River Canyon, Glen Canyon National Recreation Area, Utah.

Inspiration Point, Bryce Canyon National Park, Utah.

Green River overlook, Island in the Sky, Canyonlands National Park, Utah.

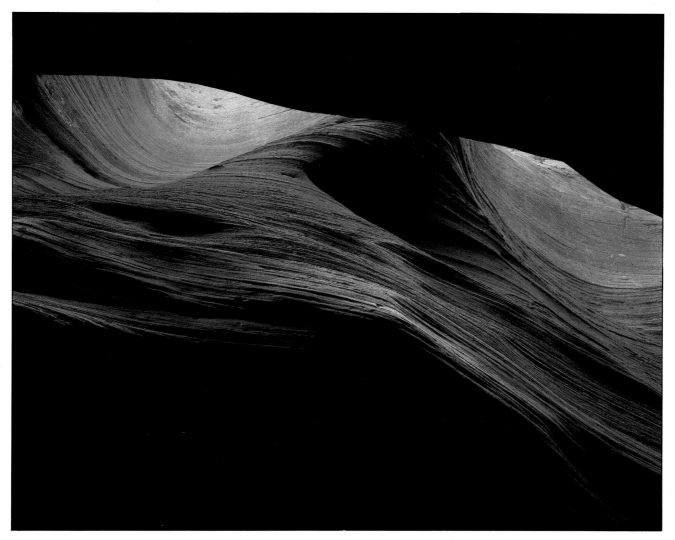

Slot canyon, Echo Canyon, East Rim Trail, Zion National Park, Utah.

Rainbow Bridge, Glen Canyon National Recreation Area, Utah.

26

Gooseneck of the Colorado, Dead Horse Point, Canyonlands National Park, Utah.

LION EYES

It was going to be a long ride home for fifteen Navajo children. Dropping kids off five, ten, and twenty miles apart is no small task. We were committed for the night. The sun had just vanished behind Giant's Knuckles, causing those in the back of the pickup to huddle close.

"It gets cold in the desert," I said.

"It's winter," one of the children replied. They covered their mouths with their hands, giggling, as we continued to bump along the dirt roads surrounding Montezuma Creek. What did the driver and I know? We were Anglos.

We had been down by the river for the afternoon. A thin veneer of ice had coalesced along its edge, and the children, bending down, would break off pieces and hold them between their thumbs and forefingers. Before the ice would melt, some brought the thin sheet to their eyes as a lens, while others placed it in their mouths and sucked on the river. Still others winged the ice sheets across the cobbles, watching, listening to them shatter like glass.

Life on the river's edge was explored through whirligig beetles, water skaters, and caddis fly larvae under stones. Canada geese flew above the channel, landing for brief intervals, then continuing on their way. The children followed tracks, expecting to meet a pack of stray dogs hiding

Ice pattern, Echo Canyon, Zion National Park, Utah.

in the tamarisks. Our shadows grew longer with the last light of day reflecting on river rapids and willows.

The hours by the river were all spent. Now, in the back of the pickup, the children told tales of days when a horse could enter a hogan and leave as a man; of skinwalkers disguised as coyotes who stalk the reservation with bones in their hands, scratching white crosses on the doors of ill-fated households. They spoke of white owls, ghostly flashes of light that could turn the blood of mice into milk.

Just then, my friend hit the brakes and those of us in the back fell forward.

"What was that?" The driver leaned his head out the window so we could hear him. "Did you see that?"

"What?" we all asked.

"A mountain lion! It streaked across the road. I'll swear it was all tail!"

The children whispered among themselves, "Mountain Lion . . ."

We filed out of the truck. My friend and I walked a few feet ahead. We found the tracks. A rosette. Five-toed pads, clawless, imprinted on the sand in spite of the cold.

"No question," I said. "Lion. I wonder where she is now?"

Looking into the darkness, I could only imagine the desert cat staring back at us. I looked over at the children; most of them were leaning against the truck as headlights approached.

"What's going on?" a local Navajo asked as he rolled down the window of his pickup with his motor idling.

My friend recognized him as the uncle of one of the children. "We think we saw a mountain lion," he said.

"Where? How long ago?"

The other man in the cab of the truck asked if we were sure.

"Pretty sure," I said. "Look at these tracks."

The men got out of their vehicle and shined their flashlights on the ground until they picked up the prints. One of the men knelt down and touched them.

"This is not good," the uncle said. "They kill our sheep." He looked into the night and then back at us. "What color of eyes did it have?"

My friend and I looked at each other. The Navajo elder began reciting the color of animals' eyes at night.

"Deer's eyes are blue. Coyote's eyes are red." His nephew interrupted him. "Green—the lion's eyes were green."

The two men said they would be back with their guns and sons tomorrow.

We returned to the truck, the driver with a handful of kids up front and the rest in the back around me as we nestled together under blankets. The children became unusually quiet, speaking in low, serious voices about why mountain lions are considered dangerous.

"It's more than just killing sheep," one child explained. "Mountain Lion is a god, one of the supernaturals that has power over us."

Each child gave away little bits of knowledge concerning the lion: that it chirps like a bird to fool you; that parts of its body are used for medicine; that in the old days, hunters used the sinew of lion for their bows. The children grew more and more anxious as fear seized their voices like two hands around their throats. They were hushed.

We traveled through the starlit desert in silence, except for the hum of the motor and four wheels flying over the washboard.

In time, from the rear of the pickup, came a slow, deliberate chant. Navajo words—gentle, deep meanderings of music born out of healing. I could not tell who had initiated the song, but one by one each child entered the melody. Over and over they sang the same monotonous notes, dreamlike at first, until gradually the cadence quickened. The children's mood began to lighten, and they swayed back and forth. What had begun as a cautious, fearful tone emerged as a joyous one. Their elders had taught them well. They had sung themselves back to hózhó, where the world is balanced and whole.

After the last child had been taken home, my friend and I were left with each other, but the echo of the children's chant remained. With many miles to go, we rolled down the windows in the cab of the truck, letting the chilled air blow through. Mountain Lion, whose eyes I did not see, lay on the mesa, her whiskers retrieving each note carried by the wind.

Wall detail, Cottonwood
Canyon near Capitol
Reef National Park,
Utah.

Valley of the Gods, Utah.

Monument Valley, Utah.

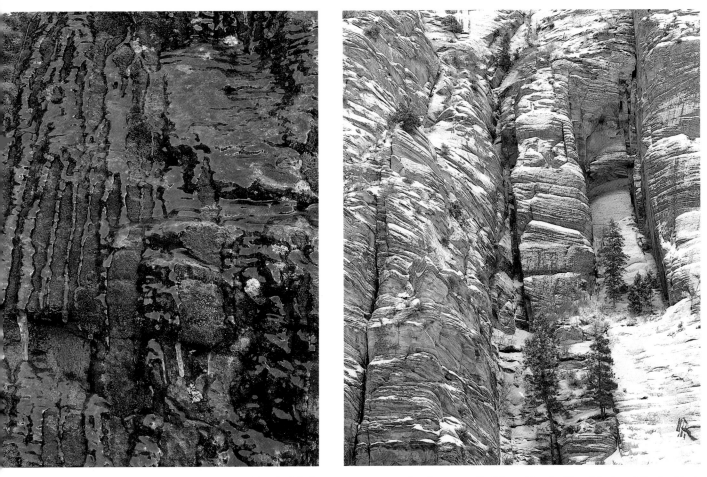

Echo Canyon, Zion National Park, Utah.   Sandstone wall, Clear Creek, Zion National Park, Utah.

THE BOWL

There was a woman who left the city, left her husband, and her children, left everything behind to retrieve her soul. She came to the desert after seeing her gaunt face in the mirror, the pallor that comes when everything is going out and nothing is coming in. She had noticed for the first time the furrows under her eyes that had been eroded by tears. She did not know the woman in the mirror. She took off her apron, folded it neatly in the drawer, left a note for her family, and closed the door behind her. She knew that her life and the lives of those she loved depended on it.

The woman returned to the place of her childhood, where she last remembered her true nature. She returned to the intimacy of a small canyon that for years had loomed large in her imagination, and there she set up camp. The walls were as she had recalled them, tall and streaked from rim to floor. The rock appeared as draped fabric as she placed her hand flat against its face. The wall was cold; the sun had not yet reached the wash. She began wading the shallow stream that ran down the center of the canyon, and chose not to be encumbered by anything. She shed her clothing, took out her hairpins, and squeezed the last lemon she had over her body. Running her hands over her breasts and throat and behind her neck, the woman shivered at her own bravery. This is

Coyote Gulch, Escalante Wilderness, Utah.

36

how it should be, she thought. She was free and frightened and beautiful.

For days, the woman wandered in and out of the slickrock maze. She drank from springs and ate the purple fruit of prickly pears. Her needs were met simply. Because she could not see herself, she was unaware of the changes—how her skin became taut and tan, the way in which her hair relaxed and curled itself. She even seemed to walk differently as her toes spread and gripped the sand.

All along the wash, clay balls had been thrown by a raging river. The woman picked one up, pulled off the pebbles until she had a mound of supple clay. She kneaded it as she walked, rubbed the clay between the palms of her hands, and watched it lengthen. She finally sat down on the moist sand and, with her fingers, continued moving up the string of clay. And then she began to coil it, around and around, pinching shut each rotation. She created a bowl.

The woman found other clay balls and put them inside the bowl. She had an idea of making dolls for her children, small clay figurines that she would let dry in the sun. Once again, she stopped walking and sat in the sand to work. She split each clay ball in two, which meant she had six small pieces to mold out of three balls she had found. One by one, tiny shapes took form. A girl with open arms above her head; three boys—one standing, one sitting, and one lying down (he was growing, she mused); and then a man and a woman facing each other. She had re-created her family. With the few scraps left over she made desert animals: a lizard, a small bird, and a miniature coyote sitting on his haunches. The woman smiled as she looked over her menagerie. She clapped her hands to remove the dried clay and half expected to see them dance. Instead, it began to rain.

Within minutes, the wash began to swell. The woman put the clay creatures into the bowl and sought higher ground up a side canyon, where she found shelter under a large overhang. She was prepared to watch if a flash flood came. And it did. The clear water turned muddy as it began to rise, carrying with it the force of wild horses running with a thunderstorm behind them. The small stream, now a river, rose higher still, gouging into the sandy banks, hurling rocks, roots, and trees down-stream. The woman wondered about the animals as she heard stirrings in the grasses and surmised they must be seeking refuge in the side canyons as she was—watching as she was. She pulled her legs in and wrapped her arms around her shins, resting her cheekbones against her knees. She closed her eyes and concentrated on the sound of water bursting through the silence of the canyon.

The roar of the flood gradually softened until it was replaced by bird-song. Swifts and swallows plucked the water for insects as frogs announced their return. The woman raised her head. With the bowl in both hands, she tried to get up, but slipped down the hillside, scraping the backs of her thighs on rabbitbrush and sage. She finally reached the wash with the bowl and its contents intact. And then she found herself with another problem: she sank up to her knees in the wet, red clay, only to find that the more she tried to pull her foot free, the deeper she sank with the other. Finally, letting go of her struggle, she put the bowl and her family aside, and wallowed in it. She fell sideways and rolled onto her stomach, then over onto her back. She was covered in slimy, wet clay, and it was delicious. She stretched her hands above her head, flexed her calves, and pointed her toes. The woman laughed hysterically until she became aware of her own echo.

Her body contracted.

She must get control of herself, she thought; what would her husband think? What kind of example was she setting for her children? And then she remembered—she was alone. She sat up and stared at the coiled bowl full of clay people. The woman took out the figurines and planted them in the wash. She placed the animals around them.

"They're on their own," she said out loud. And she walked back to the spring where she had drunk, filled up her bowl with water, and bathed.

The next morning, when the woman awoke, she noticed that the cottonwood branches swaying above her head had sprouted leaves.

She could go home now.

Escalante River, Escalante Wilderness, Utah.

Hidden Canyon, Zion National Park, Utah.

Grotto, Zion National Park, Utah.

Stevens Canyon, Escalante Wilderness, Utah.

Virginia creeper and sandstone boulders, Stevens Canyon, Escalante, Utah.

Wall with box elder trees,
Kolob Canyon,
Zion National Park, Utah.

Wall detail, Neon Canyon, Escalante, Utah.

46

Valley of the Gods, Utah.

BURIED POEMS

There is a man in Boulder, Utah, who buries poems in the desert. He is an archaeologist who knows through his profession that eventually his words will be excavated, that although they may not be understood now by his community, at a later date his poetry will be held as an artifact, mulled over by minds that will follow his.

This man is alone, walled in by the wilderness he loves and neighbors who don't understand him. They say he spends too much time with the dead, that his loyalties are to bones, that the land could be better used for the planting of corn than the digging of corpses. They say he talks too little and thinks too much for a town like Boulder.

He has lived among the locals for decades, but he is still an outsider. It is the Anasazi who keep him here. They are his neighbors, the ones who court his imagination. It is their echoes reverberating through the canyons that hold him.

He listens and he studies. He pores over the artifacts that come into the museum where he works. When no one is around, he pulls out his glasses, slips on his white cotton gloves, and carefully turns the objects over and over as though some wisdom might speak to him from a sandal or basket or cradle board.

Occasionally, a local or two drop in. He invites them outdoors and encourages them to sit between sage. He takes his hand and sweeps it

Capitol Gorge, Capitol Reef National Park, Utah.

across the valley and tells them this site was once occupied by over two hundred individuals, continuously from A.D. 1050 to 1200, that this is twice the population living in Boulder today. He tells them the Anasazi were born farmers, and hunters and gatherers—planting beans, squash, and corn as they supplemented their diet with big game and rodents. He tries to convince them that the Anasazi, through their technology of manos, metates, pinched pots, and atlatls, were remarkable people well adapted to an inhospitable environment. And then he stops himself, realizing how carried away he has become. He lets the visitors wander among the ruins.

On another day, some neighbors ask, "Are you finding anything good out there?"

"It's all good," the archaeologist replies, "corn cobs, charcoal, and chipping debris. . . ."

The neighbors are unimpressed. He gives in.

"But one time, we were excavating in a particular site and uncovered three ollas—corrugated vessels used for carrying water. Next to these pots were two large balls of clay that had been kneaded. You could still see palm marks from the anonymous hands that had made them. Beneath the pots and clay balls was a burial, the delicate placement of female bones."

He pauses as he rubs his hand over the soil. "I honestly believe she was a potter. We have found no reference to anything like it in the literature. It is most unusual."

The locals look at him, puzzled, and shake their heads. It doesn't register. He sees it in their eyes. They ask him for evidence and he says they buried it for another generation to uncover. They look at the dry land and they look at him, and they walk away.

The man leaves the museum for the day, locks the door behind him, and retreats to his spot in the rocks. He pulls out his pencil and spiral notebook from a front pocket of his cowboy shirt and begins writing. Poems come to him like wild horses to water. He writes a few lines, tears the paper, and burns the edges with his lighter. He writes another verse, tears it from his notebook, antiques it with fire, and places it in a pile that he holds down with his boot. By the end of the afternoon, he has a dozen or more poems. On his way home, he buries them.

The man knows the ways of these people. They ranch and they farm. They know the contours of the land, and if a white triangle of paper is sprouting where corn should be, they'll pull it up. Or if the cows are out grazing and happen to kick a sheet of paper into the air, it'll get read by the wranglers. And when women are planting borders of zinnias around their homes and uncover a poem with their trowel, they'll call their neighbors just to pass the words along.

Which is exactly what happened. Within a matter of days, the whole town of Boulder was reading each other poetry.

Some think they are love poems written by an Indian. Others guess they are clues to a buried treasure left by John Wesley Powell or Father Escalante. And still others believe they are personal messages left especially for them by a deceased family member, which is how they became known as "the ghost poems."

The archaeologist listens. He walks about town with his hands in his pockets. People are talking across fences, over melon stands, and inside

San Rafael River Canyon from Wedge overlook, San Rafael Swell, Utah.

Bentonite Hills, Capitol Reef National Park, Utah.

their automobiles. Some individuals are even offering to buy them from their friends. But the finders of the poems won't sell. The man who buries the poems quietly slips into the convenience store and buys another notebook and lighter and returns to his place in the rocks.

His poems become shorter, more cryptic, until, finally, they are a series of pictographs — the pictographs found in Calf Creek Canyon, Coyote Gulch and Mimi's Grotto.

The town eventually seeks him out, asking if he knows what these picture poems might mean. He refers them to different canyons, invites them to his slide shows, and tells them stories about the Anasazi who once lived where they do now. He explains how these drawings on canyon walls are a reflection of Anasazi culture, of rituals, and all that mattered in their lives. Now, he tells them, we can only speculate. The townsfolk are listening. He sees it in their eyes.

A local hands him a poem and says, "Read this. My boy found it buried near the overhang behind our ranch."

The archaeologist reads the poem out loud.

SOUNDS

The ruin clings to the cliff

Under the arching sandstone.

It is quiet now.

No longer do you hear the laughter,

The everyday sounds:

Women making pottery—the slap, slap of clay,

People cooking,

Men returning from the hunt,

The builders,

Children playing,

The cries of sorrow when a loved one passes on.

They are gone now—

The Anasazi.

The survivors.

The adaptors.

The only sounds now

Are those of the wind

The raucous sound of the raven, and

The descending sound of the canyon wren.

The guardians.

Poem by Larry Davis, an archaeologist in Boulder, Utah.

By now, the town of Boulder has hundreds of these poems in its possession. They hang in the schoolhouse, where the children are taking

Slot canyon in Navajo sandstone near Page, Arizona.

Hanging Arch, Stevens Canyon, Escalante Wilderness, Utah.

Anasazi pictographs, Grand Gulch, Utah.

up the mystery. The community still wonders who is responsible for these writings, questioning just how long they will continue to be found. But poems keep appearing in the strangest places: in milk cans, on tractor seats, church pews, and irrigation ditches. And rumor has it, the canyons are filled with them. It just may be that the man who buries poems in the desert has turned the whole damned town into archaeologists. The next thing we'll hear is that the locals want to preserve the wilderness for its poetry.

KOKOPELLI'S RETURN

One night, beneath the ruins of Keet Seel, we heard flute music—music so sweet it could have split the seeds of corn. Earlier we had wandered through the rooms of Keet Seel, admiring the redrock construction dabbed into the sandstone alcove like swallows' nests, but there had been no music then—only the silence pressing against us in the cool Anasazi air.

Above the ruins, clouds covered the full face of the moon like gauze. The land seemed to bow with the melody of the flute. I reached for my husband's arm and he reached for our friend. We kept hold of one another like children, and we listened, holding our breaths between the intervals of our own heartbeats. The flute music flowed out from the cliff dwelling like an ancient breath.

The next morning we sat around camp, drinking rose hip tea. We were tired and stiff from the cold, still half stunned from the night before. Our friend, who was Hopi, looked down at the cup he held in both hands, and told a story.

A man traveled through this country with a bag of corn seed over one shoulder. His shadow against the desert looked like a deformity. He would stop at every village and teach the people how to plant corn. And then when the sun slipped behind the mesa and the village was asleep, he would walk through the cornfields playing his

Double Arch alcove, Kolob Canyon, Zion National Park, Utah.

60

flute. The seeds would flower, pushing themselves up through the red, sandy soil and follow the high-pitched notes upward. The sun would rise and the man would be gone, with corn stalks the height of a young girl shimmering in the morning light. Many of the young women would complain of a fullness in their bellies. The elders would smile, knowing they were pregnant. They would look to the southwest and call him "Kokopelli."

We finished our tea, broke up our camp, and organized our packs for the trail. Before leaving, I walked back to the base of Keet Seel. The ruins appeared darker than usual, full of shadows that moved from room to room. My eyes followed the tall timbers from floor to ceiling as I imagined macaws perched on top. Kivas held darkness below, and I wondered if old men's bones might be buried there. Just then, in a stream of light, a pictograph on the ceiling of the alcove jumped out. It was a buglike creature, but as I focused more clearly I recognized it as the humpbacked flute player.

"Kokopelli," I whispered to myself. "It must be Kokopelli."

The light shifted and he seemed to be rocking on his back. I had missed him the day before, noticing only the pictographs of bighorn sheep and spirals. At that moment, I recalled the flute music that flooded the canyon the night before and the clouds like gossamer hands with long, long fingers that pulled me into an abyss of sleep. I placed my hand over my stomach, turned away from the ruins, and walked back toward my fellow campers. Halfway down the canyon, I felt stirrings in my belly. Sweet corn was sprouting all along the river.

Walls and seeps with cactus, Cottonwood Canyon, Glen Canyon National Recreation Area, Utah.

Choprock Canyon, Escalante, Utah.

Cottonwood Canyon, Glen Canyon National Recreation Area, Utah.

65

Betatakin Ruin, Navajo National Monument, Arizona.

Neon Canyon, Escalante, Utah.

Wall detail, Moki Canyon, Glen Canyon National Recreation Area.

PERFECT KIVA

In a poorly lit corner of a restaurant in Moab, a woman draws a map on a napkin and slips it to a man. The man studies the paper square carefully and asks her a few questions. He thanks her. They pay for their meals and then part ways.

The man stops at a gas station, fills up his truck, then walks to the corner pay phone and makes three calls. Within hours, he meets five friends in Blanding, Utah, at the Rainbow Cafe. They conspire under the plastic jade lanterns, eating Navajo tacos and egg rolls.

"It's called Perfect Kiva. We'll camp on top of the mesa tonight, then hike into the canyon tomorrow. The site is on our right, up high, the third ledge down. I have the map."

The six left Blanding in three trucks. The man with the map led them in the dark across miles of dirt roads that crisscrossed the mesa. In a sense, he had blindfolded them. That was his plan, and his promise to the woman in Moab.

Their camp appeared as a black hole in the desert. Each person drew out his flashlight and checked the ground for cow pies and scorpions. One by one, they threw down their sleeping bags and fell asleep. Dream time was kept by the rotation of stars.

Anasazi cliff dwelling, Grand Gulch, Utah.

68

Dawn came into the country like a secret. The six had burrowed so deep inside their bags that they emerged like startled ground squirrels after an eight-hour hibernation. The black hole of the previous night had been transformed into a bevy of piñon and juniper. A few yards beyond was a cut in the desert a quarter mile wide.

Camp was erased. Cars were locked. Water bottles were filled and packs put on. The pacing was brisk as they descended into one of the finger canyons. For two hours, they walked in and out of morning shadows, until, finally, they stood on the slickrock in full sunlight.

The man with the map studied cliffs, looking for the perfect alcove with the perfect kiva. Placing their trust in the leader, the others kept walking and found pleasures in small things like blister beetles and feathers snatched from the air by sage. The desert heat loosened the muscles and spirit of the group. Joy crept in and filled their boots. A few ran up and down boulders just to see if their courage could hold them. Others focused on birds—a lazuli bunting here, an ash-throated flycatcher there. But the man with the map kept looking.

A raven flew out from the rocks.

"There it is!" cried the leader. "The third ledge down. I'll bet that's our alcove."

The six began to climb where the raven flew. They hiked straight up, some on hands and knees, through the sandstone scree, until finally, breathless, they encountered the ruins. Upright and stable, in spite of the thousand feet below them, the friends stood in wonder. They had entered an open-sided hallway of stone. Pink stone. Stone so soft that if held it would crumble.

70

There were figures with broad shoulders and wild eyes staring at them from inside the rock—petroglyphs that not only seized the imagination but turned it upside down. Animals with bear bodies and deer heads danced on the overhang. Walls made of dry-laid stones divided the ledge. Most of them had tumbled with time: no mortar had been used, just the careful placement of stone against stone to house the Anasazi.

Beyond the walls were mealing bins, standing stones that corraled the corn. The manos and metates were gone, but images of women chanting corn to meal were as real as the shriveled cobs piled inside the granary.

Perfect Kiva was more subtle. It was recognizable only by the fraying juniper bark that had shown through the eroded sand. The six sat outside the circle until calm. The kiva seemed to ask that of them. Five slabs of sandstone framed the entrance, which appeared as a dark square on the ledge floor. A juniper ladder with rungs of willow led to the underworld. They paused. The ladder that had supported the Ancient Ones might not support them. They chose not to use it. Instead, they jerry-rigged a sling out of nylon cording and caribiners and anchored it around a boulder. They moved the ladder aside and, one by one, lowered themselves into the kiva. Perfect Kiva—round like the earth. Hidden in the earth, the six sat.

It took a few minutes for their eyes to adjust. Cobwebs dangled from the wooden ceiling, most likely black widows spinning webs off the cribbed logs and pilasters. Walls bricked, then plastered, created the smooth red circumference of the ceremonial chamber. Four shelves were cut into the walls. Each was lined with juniper lace and berries. Two full moons, one green and one white, faced each other on the east and west walls. A green

71

serpent of the same pigment moved on the north wall, west to east, connecting the circles.

No one spoke. The six remained captive to their own meanderings, each individual absorbing what he was in need of. An angle of light poured through the hole in the ceiling as the dust in the air danced up the ladder. They breathed deeply. It was old, old air.

The longer they sat in the kiva, the more they saw. There was a hearth in the center, a smoke vent to the south, eight loom anchors, and the fine desert powder they were sitting on. But the focus inside the kiva was on the sipapu—the small hole in the floor that, according to Hopi myth, promised emergence. In time, each one circled the sipapu with his fingers and raised himself on the slings. They untied the rope from around the boulder and placed the Anasazi ladder back where it had been for as long as ravens had a memory.

A few months later, in a poorly lit corner of a restaurant in Moab, a woman speaks softly to a man.

"They took the ladder, put it in a museum, and stabilized the kiva. It's just not the same," she whispers. "They fear aging and want it stopped like an insect in amber."

He studies her face and asks her a few questions. He thanks her. They pay for their meals and then part ways.

The man stops at a gas station, fills up his truck, then walks to the corner pay phone and makes three calls. Within hours, the six meet in Blanding at the Rainbow Cafe.

"It's called theft in the name of preservation," he says. "The ladder is held hostage at the local museum. It belongs to the desert. It must be returned."

The friends move closer around the table.

"Tomorrow—," he says.

"Tonight," they insist.

Dawn came into the country like a secret.

Wall detail, Glen Canyon National Recreation Area.

73

Erosion wash, Stevens Canyon, Escalante, Utah.

Grandview Pointe, Island in the Sky, Canyonlands National Park, Utah.

San Juan River at Honaker Trail, Bluff, Utah.

Forgotten Canyon, Glen Canyon National Recreation Area, Utah.

Anasazi cliff dwelling, Grand Gulch, Utah.

Cottonwood Canyon, Glen Canyon National Recreation Area, Utah.

A WOMAN'S DANCE

She came to the desert to dance. The woman gathered a variety of plants: mullen, sage, chamisa, mint, Oregon grape, aster, equisetum, and yarrow. She carried them in the folds of her long, red skirt to a clearing. It was a meadow defined by juniper. She placed the plants in the center and returned to the trees. She took off her paisley bandana wrapped around her forehead and knelt on the red soil.

"Good death," she said, as her hands sifted the wood dust of a decaying tree. She opened her scarf and placed the henna wood chips on the silk square. After she had gathered enough for the task, she brought the four corners together, tied them, and walked back to the clearing. She was not alone. Flickers, robins, magpies, and jays accompanied her. The woman carefully untied one of the corners and let the wood dust sprinkle to the ground as she walked in a circle. Next, she retrieved the plants from the center and arranged them end to end on top of the wood dust to define her circle more clearly. She liked what she saw.

Movement surrounded her. The wind, clouds, grasses, and birds—all reminded her that nothing stands still. She held up the hem of her skirt in both hands and began walking briskly around the circle. Deep breaths took the aroma of mint and sage down to her toes. Her long, spirited stride broke into short leaps with extended arms as she entered

Slot canyon near Page, Arizona.

the circle dancing, without guile, without notice, without any thought of herself. She danced from the joy of all she was a part.

Pronghorn Antelope entered the circle through her body. She danced Eagle, Raven, and Bear. The Four Seasons sent her swirling as she danced to ignite the Moon. She danced until gravity pulled her down, and then she rested, her eyes closed, with nothing moving but her heart and lungs, beating, breathing, against the hot, dry desert.

With her ear against the earth, the woman listened. A chant began to rise. Slowly, she raised her body like a lizard. An audience had gathered. Each individual sat cross-legged around the plant circle with a found instrument: rocks, bones, sticks, stumps, whistles, and voices. For hours, they played music, organic and whole, as she danced. Her hands, like serpents, encouraged primal sounds as she arched forward and back with the grasses. She was the wind that inspired change. They were a tribe creating a landscape where lines between the real and imagined were thinly drawn.

The light deepened, shadows lengthened, and the woman began to turn. Her turns widened with each rotation until she stopped, perfectly balanced. The woman stepped outside the circle and kissed the palms of her hands and placed them on the earth. The dance was over.

The audience rose, refreshed. Each picked up one of the plants that held the circle and took a handful of wood dust to scatter, leaving no clues in the clearing of ever having been there. They disappeared as mysteriously as they had arrived.

And the woman who came to the desert to dance simply ran her fingers through her long, black hair and smiled.

Gambel oak and sacred datura, Llewellyn Gulch, Glen Canyon National Recreation Area, Utah.

Near Oak Canyon, Glen Canyon National Recreation Area, Utah.

Streaked sandstone, Valley of Fire State Park, Nevada.

Box Elder Campground, Dinosaur National Monument, Colorado

Moonrise, Temple of the Moon, Cathedral Valley, Capitol Reef National Park, Utah.

Needles Overlook, Canyonlands National Park, Utah.

THE STONE SPIRAL

They gathered stones along the river. Dark to light. It was a game at first, something to move along a slow afternoon. But once they began to see all the colors of the riverbed, the spectrum of stones became an obsession. Blacks were easy, so were whites. Shades of red were plentiful—after all, they were the sandstones that made up the country. Green stones shattered from limestone appeared foreign and exotic, as did lavenders and blues from slate and shale. Brown and yellow stones were harder to find—the sulphur and quartz most people take for granted. They piled the rocks on the sand like a stash of old billiard balls.

After the various hues had been selected in all their gradations, the man and the woman began to create a spiral. Together they lifted a large, black river cobble and placed it in the center. It was smooth and polished and elegant. Next to the black stone was a not-so-black stone, five stones down a charcoal one, next to it, deep purple. Then came the blue stones: navy, cobalt, teal, and turquoise. An olive stone carried the spectrum to yellow, orange, red-orange, maroon, indigo, lavender, pale pink, and white. The spiral wound around the flood plain like a coiled snake.

After the spiral was complete, they walked around it (some adjustments were made), talking themselves through each stone and color. They began to tell stories about the creation of the world, how this stone ruled the sky and this stone ruled the forest and this one the sea. They picked

Autumn leaves on pool, Emerald Pools, Zion National Park, Utah.

guardian stones for animals and birds, insects, and spiders. The black center stone became Black Widow's domain. They imagined her underneath, spinning the web, binding them all together.

The light began to change. The temperature seemed to drop, and the river was slowing down as if the mountain snows had given enough of themselves that day. The sun was disappearing behind a mesa. Reflected light bouncing off canyon walls intensified the colors until even human skin appeared burnished and bronzed.

Welcoming twilight, the couple began hurling small white pebbles into the sky, ducking at first so they wouldn't be hit, and then laughing, crying out loud, "First star, second star, third star, fourth. . . ." And then another game ensued. They found themselves lying on the riverbank counting stars. It surprised them how long it really took for the night sky to be lit. An hour after sunset only one hundred stars had appeared. But as the man and the woman turned to each other, the stars began to double and triple exponentially, until the Milky Way draped over them. By this time, the lovers drifted in and out of sleep until dawn.

When they awoke, the stars were gone. They found themselves covered with leaves. But their stone spiral was still intact. The stones were pale. The man and woman pretended the stones were thirsty, and walked down to the river. With cupped hands they returned to the rocks with water; again and again, they let the stones drink. They seemed to blush and gurgle and shine. The spectrum of colored stones was revived.

The sun had moved to midsky as the couple sat among the stones and spoke of family. With willow sticks they wrote the names of mothers, fathers, brothers, sisters, cousins, aunts and uncles, grandmothers and grandfathers in the soft sand outside the spiral. They flirted with each other, saying between the two of them their relatives could fill the desert. Standing up, they recognized what extraordinary clans they belonged to.

With no more thought than a flock of birds gives to flight, the man and woman leaped from stone to stone. Taking hold of one another's hands, with great joy, they entered the current and floated, like a wish, downriver.

Emerald Pools, Zion National Park, Utah.

Seven Mile Canyon, Glen Canyon National Recreation Area, Utah.

Autumn trees and Virgin River, Temple of Sinawava, Zion National Park, Utah.

Choprock Canyon, Escalante, Utah.

Sandstone erosion and water pockets, Stevens Canyon, Escalante, Utah.

Virgin River, Zion Narrows, Zion National Park, Utah.

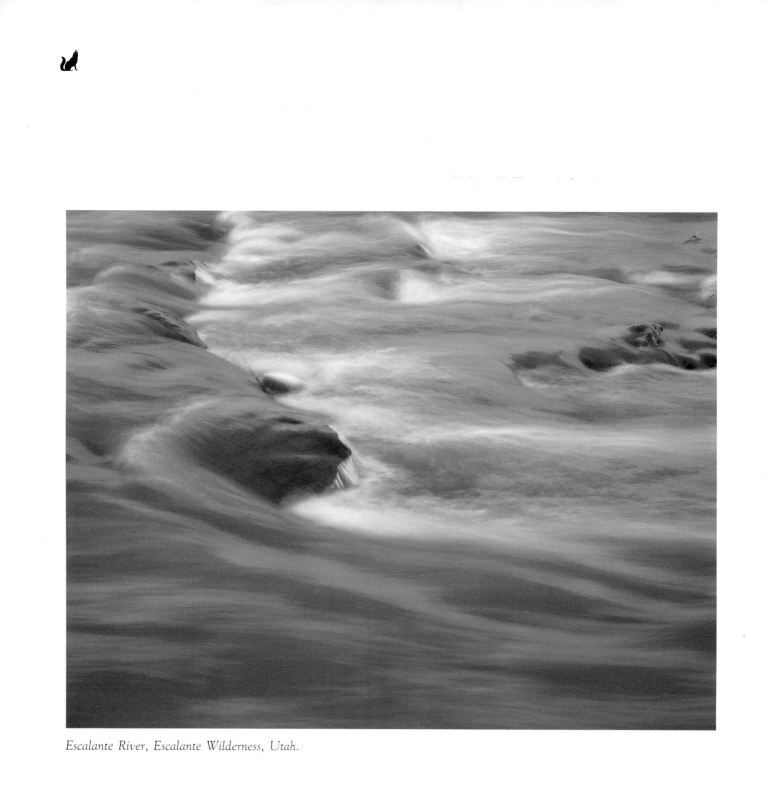

Escalante River, Escalante Wilderness, Utah.